COLORS IN FRENCH

BLUE IN FRENCH

BLEUE

BLACK
IN FRENCH
NOIRE

YELLOW

IN FRENCH

JAUNE

GRAY IN FRENCH

GRIS

ORANGE
IN FRENCH
ORANGE

BROWN

IN FRENCH

MARRON

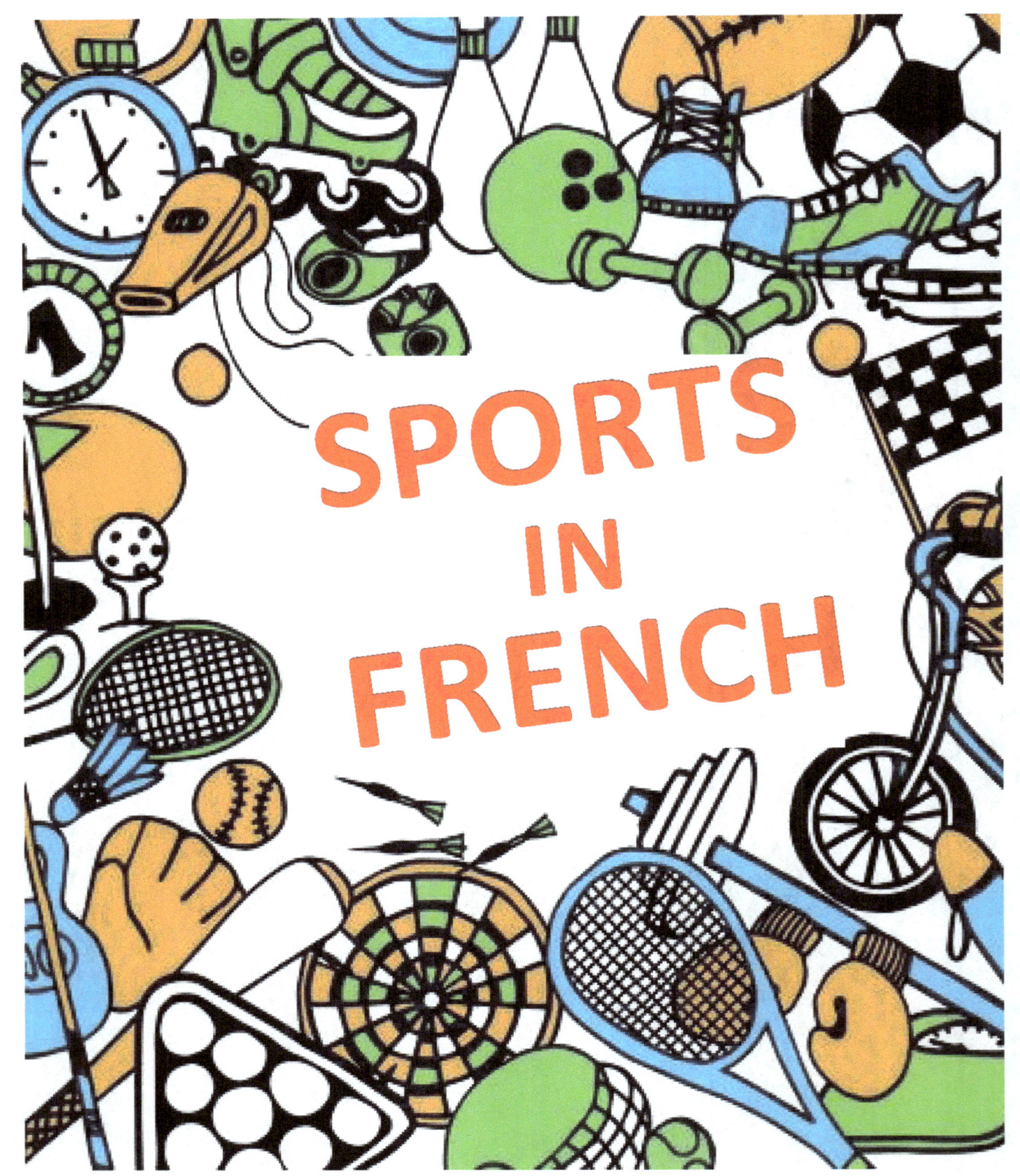

FOOTBALL
IN FRENCH
FOOTBALL

BASEBALL IN FRENCH
BASE-BALL

BOXING
IN FRENCH
BOXE

TENNIS
IN FRENCH
TENNIS

BASKETBALL
IN FRENCH

BASKETTEUR

ICE HOCKEY
IN FRENCH
HOCKEY SUR GLACE

SOCCER
IN FRENCH
FOOTBALL

TRACK THE SPORT

IN FRENCH

SUIVEZ LE SPORT